Productivity

How to Focus and Stay Productive

Stop Procrastination Now

and Improve Yourself!

By Edwin Lee

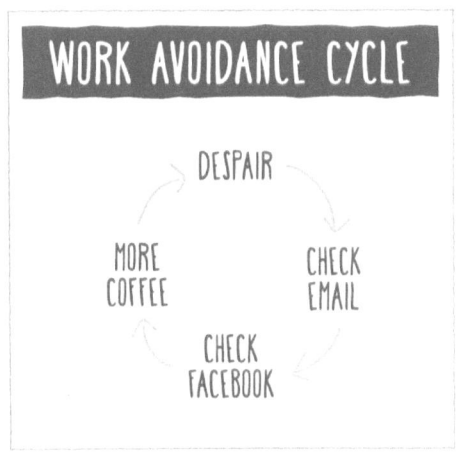

Seems familiar?

Sometimes this applies even into the work we'd actually like to get done.

Introduction

I want to thank you for purchasing this *"Productivity guide"*

This book has powerful information that, if followed, can help you become more focused, productive, and successful in every area of life. Remember mastering these things will require some time and effort.

We all have various tasks to attend to every day and certain goals we would like to manifest in our lives. Doing any of these requires that we have a perfect blend of laser focus, strong sense of self-discipline, and good time management skills so we can do our tasks attentively, make sure we do not succumb to the temptations that keep us from doing meaningful things, and so that we can make the most efficient and effective use of our time. Unless we work on these things, we are very poorly equipped to beat procrastination and increase our productivity.

To eliminate the innate need to defer your important work to a later time and to ensure you manage your distractions effectively and in so doing, complete all your work on time, you need to overcome procrastination and improve your time management skills.

If this is something you would like to achieve, this book is the complete productivity guide. When implemented, the information in this book will help increase your level of focus and skyrocket your productivity in a matter of days and in the end, we focus on the long-term results. I've also included guidance for your next step on how to form a habit out of this.

Are you ready to become the most productive person you know? If you are, let's get started. If you aren't, STOP procrastinating...! We are starting.

I'm glad you decided to give this book a shot. I wanted to keep it short so you can seriously recall most of the advice given here. I hope you enjoy it and actually focus while reading so you'll know how to make the progress properly.

owned by the owners themselves, not affiliated with this document.

Table of Contents

Introduction

The Relationship between Success, Laser Focus, Self-Discipline, and Good Time Management

How Sharp Focus, Self-Discipline, Good Time Management and Resilience Help You Become Productive and Successful

Step 1: Build the Determination to Be Productive

How to Become Determined to Increase Your Focus and Productivity

Step 2: Plan Your Work

How Planning Increases your Productivity

How to Plan and Prioritize Your Work

Step 3: Fight the Urge to Procrastinate

The Relationship between Success, Laser Focus, Self-Discipline, and Good Time Management

Whether your goal is to keep your house spick and span, spend quality time with your kids and raise them in a good environment, or to become the CEO of your company and make it extremely successful or anything else, to achieve your objective, you need to be extremely focused, disciplined, efficient, and productive.

Sharp focus, self-discipline, good time management, and resilience are the main characteristics of the highly productive and successful. You may be wondering, "how and what does this mean?"

Let us find that out before we move to discussing strategies guaranteed to help you become super productive and successful:

How Sharp Focus, Self-Discipline, Good Time Management and Resilience Help You Become Productive and Successful

To achieve success, whatever way you choose to define it, the key things you need to be are *highly focused and immensely disciplined.* If you are not hawk-like focused on what you want to achieve and lack the discipline to keep doing what is important, you are likely to fall prey to distraction, jump from one task to another, and thus, end up achieving nothing substantive.

If you fail to exercise complete focus on what you want to achieve, and are not strong enough to say no to distractions, you are likely to stay idle all day long, do meaningless stuff or hang out with friends whenever they call you, or do anything and everything that steers you away from your goal.

Moreover, when you fail to focus on your goal and lack enough self-control, you are likely to be less resilient and practice bad time management too. If you are not determined to achieve your goal, say, for instance, your goal is to win gold at a swimming competition, you are likely to lose hope when you lose a certain competition and start feeling as if you lack what it takes to actualize your goal.

Moreover, a lack of focus and self-discipline also make it easier to give in to procrastination and waste your time instead of using it efficiently. Instead of differentiating high priority tasks from low priority ones and working on tasks that skyrocket your productivity, you are likely to do things that lower your productivity.

When you lack focus and self-discipline, building resilience and staying productive is nearly impossible because temptations and the tendency to prioritize instant gratification over delayed gratification makes it difficult for you to stay strong in difficult times, do what you have to do, keep moving forward, and work on high priority tasks first. In fact, a lack of focus and self-discipline is why you fail to achieve any of your goals and build for yourself the life you really want to live.

Fortunately, this situation is one you can reverse. If you start working on developing killer focus and self-discipline, you can slowly bring the following changes into your life and that too, for good.

1. Strong focus and self-discipline find strong rooting ground in motivation. To do something with complete success and to keep off temptations so that you can do what is important, the first thing you need is the motivation to do that task. To be motivated towards something, you need to feel connected to what you want to do. Therefore, as you seek to build focus, the first thing you have to do is establish a goal/s that hold(s) a lot of meaning to you. A meaningful goal increases your enthusiasm to fight your temptations and battle your distractions so you can stay focused on what matters.

2. Moreover, the ability to say no to temptations and focus on the bigger picture also helps you overcome procrastination. When you overcome

procrastination, you can utilize your time efficiently. When you know you must achieve something, you start making sacrifices for it and completing important tasks on time, which consequently increases your output.

3. Laser focus and discipline also keep you strong in the face of adversity. Even when troubles surround you, you know what you want and you do not stop until you get it.

All these positive changes make sure you keep moving towards your goal, whatever it may be, and eventually grab it by the neck. This ability always helps you stay productive in life, which then ensures you accomplish every goal you set.

Now that you know why you need focus, discipline, and productivity in your life, the rest of this book shall discuss various strategies that can help you become hawk-like focused, seal-like disciplined, and ant-like productive.

The first strategy of the lot is to become determined to be productive and set your intention to do so. The next section is a deep conversation about how to do this:

Step 1: Build the Determination to Be Productive

To become productive and focused, you need to beat procrastination and build self-discipline. To do that, you need to build the determination and enthusiasm to do so; these two things come from being motivated to do something.

For instance, if you are completely stimulated and excited to pursue an MBA while still holding a day job, you will attend evening classes at the University even after feeling exhausted after your day job. In this case, you will be willing to do everything it takes to juggle the two responsibilities successfully. However, if you are not motivated to do so, and studying for an MBA is not on your bucket list, you will not feel intimately motivated to study after a hectic day at work and will indeed miss many classes too.

Determination to do something comes from feeling superiorly motivated to achieve a certain goal. When you are super eager to do something, or know that from doing something, you will achieve a certain benefit or a number of benefits that mean a lot to you, you become truly committed to doing things that can help you accomplish that goal. As such, to become productive, focused, and to beat procrastination, the first thing you need to do is become determined to do so and figure out the one or few things that you really want to do so you can develop the enthusiasm you need to battle your temptations.

Let's discuss how you can become determined to increase your focus and productivity next.

How to Become Determined to Increase Your Focus and Productivity

Here is how you can do that:

1. First, examine your current way of life and think of the things you would like to change about your current life. Do you want to stop being lazy? Do you want to increase your level of organization? Do you want to complete all your tasks on time? Do you want to reduce the chaos in your life? Write down everything you want to change about your life.

2. Next, find out exactly what you want to do in your life and the goals you would like to achieve. You could have one big goal or different goals for different aspects of your life such as health, wealth, profession, happiness, relationships, spirituality, etc. For instance, your home-related goal could be to keep your house cleaner and your professional goal could be to increase your company's sales from 100 products sold in

a month to about 500. Write down the many goals you have in your mind and those that you would like to achieve and then pick any one or two you would like to work on first because simultaneously managing and achieving a couple of goals is a tad difficult and the very thing that breeds a lack of focus and productivity.

3. Think of all the reasons why you want to fulfill a certain goal. If your goal is to enroll for, and study for an MBA while still holding a day job, think of why you want to do so and the benefits having an MBA shall add to your life. Write down as many benefits of achieving your respective goal as you can think of. Make those reasons as compelling as you can. For instance, if you want to study for an MBA while managing your current job because you want to get a better paying job, write down why you want to earn more money. Explain your current difficult situation and financial crisis in depth and use it to create compelling reasons why you need to pursue your goal.

4. Read those reasons a few times aloud; you will notice feeling more compelled to follow your goal and accomplish it.

5. To increase your motivation, imagine the life you will build and the amazing feeling you will enjoy when you finally accomplish your goal. Visualize yourself accomplishing your goal and keep thinking of that proud moment for about 10 to 15 minutes.

6. Now write down how you feel about your goal. You are likely to jot down positive things about it. Write down your commitment to pursue that goal and use it to become more productive and focused in life. It is very important that you go through this commitment daily, once in the morning, and once before going to bed so you wake up feeling focused and remind yourself of your goal before sleeping.

7. Use the previous points and start to experiment and developing an enjoyable morning routine focused to help you to tackle the day. Depending on your current conditions you want to experiment yourself so I'll only give really basic ideas:

Bob: Goes to work at 7:00am Monday-Friday. Example routine; wake up 5:30am. Remember written goals, be excited, think of something positive, meditate, exercise, eat healthy breakfast.

Jane: Goes to work at 10:00am and 1:00pm. Wake up 6:00am. Remember written goals, be excited, think of something positive, cardio, gym, eat healthy breakfast or fasting.

Now that you are more committed to being productive and beating procrastination, and now that you know exactly what you need to focus on, your next step is the planning phase. The next section talks about this.

*"Productivity is just not about doing more. It is about creating more impact with less work." — **Anonymous***

Productivity is definitely not just about doing more work. In fact, some people who do a lot of work are some of the most unproductive people on earth.

The difference between a highly productive and an unproductive person is not just the amount of work they do but also the efficient use of time the former makes. Someone who is not highly productive is likely to focus on a lot of things at once and instead of doing high priority tasks first, may begin with something easier and less meaningful.

A productive and focused person will do the opposite: he/she will figure out the tasks that can increase his/her productivity and then work on these tasks first instead of doing what seems easy. That is exactly what helps him/her create the most impact.

To ensure you do the right tasks first, tasks that really help you move towards your goal and fulfill it, you need to plan your work long before you start doing it.

How Planning Increases your Productivity

A major reason why your productivity is low and why you lack focus is the mere fact that instead of doing what is important, you jump from one task to another and do things without understanding their impact. Since you have not planned how you intend to achieve your goal, you haphazardly do whatever is in front of you throughout the day without considering whether that task shall help you achieve your goal.

Creating a plan of action helps you know what you need to do to fulfill your goal and thus, reverses this and lets you know the meaningful, substantial, and high priority tasks you need to complete first to increase your productivity. With a plan in hand, you will know what to do, when to do it and how to do it, and will feel a lot more focused and clear of mind than ever.

Here is how you can plan your work.

How to Plan and Prioritize Your Work

1. First, peg your goal to a reasonable deadline. If your goal is to move to a new house, figure out how much time it will take you to pack your stuff and make the move without taking any time off from your job. If your goal is to write your first mystery novel, think of how much time you need to accomplish this task. This ensures you stay on track and by so doing, avoid procrastinating.

2. A big goal, even if it spreads over a month, can feel overwhelming especially if the goal is one you have never tackled before. If you have never written a book, the mere thought of it is very likely to overwhelm you at an emotional level. To eliminate the element of 'overwhelm' from your goal so it seems more doable and manageable to

you, break that big goal into a few smaller milestones. If your goal spreads over 6 months, break it into two smaller milestones of 3 months each, and then take the first milestone of the two and divide it into even smaller milestones. If your plan is to write a 50,000-word eBook, divide it into goals such as write 25,000 words first and break that down into write the first 15,000 words and chop thus further into writing 7,500 words. When you have smaller, bite-sized pieces of the goal in front of you, working on that goal instantly seems a lot more doable.

3. Think of how you shall accomplish the first tiny piece. What could you do to achieve it successfully and efficiently? For instance, if you want to write 5,000 words of your book in a week, find out how you can do this within the deadline. What are the different tasks you should do and those you should not to ensure you stay on track and achieve your goal as planned? Here, you need to think of the high priority and substantial tasks that can skyrocket your productivity. Think of the tasks that, if you

do, can help you achieve more in less time. For instance, if you have to do laundry, write your book, and prepare week-long meals for your family, you could dry clean your clothes and use the freed up time to work on your book so you accomplish your goal on time or even before that. You can then use the extra time to edit the work you have done thus far.

4. After determining high priority tasks, make sure you do at least 2 of them every day of the week. If a certain high priority task is difficult and demands more time, do only 1 high priority task a day.

5. Moreover, put creative tasks first on your list. According to David Rock, a popular author and co-founder of the NeuroLeadership Institute, most of us are in the habit of attending to mindless and meaningless work first and then investing our effort on the tough and more important tasks when we are already tired. This drains your energy, decreases your focus, and keeps you from creating more impact. Each decision you make tires your

brain. Therefore, if you do many pointless tasks first, you are quite likely to feel exhausted when it is time for you to do something important. To become more productive and create better impact, reverse the order of your tasks. Do tasks that require better focus and creativity immediately after getting started with your work and move to the easier stuff such as scheduling meeting or deleting useless emails from your inbox later in the day. For instance, if you have to create an agenda for your next project, do not keep that task for later in the day; instead, complete this task first thing in the morning because such a task is a creative task, one that if done right, can increase your productivity by manifolds.

6. Always set a deadline for all your tasks so you know exactly when they are due.

7. Also, set a day or two for doing the less important tasks. Some tasks such as cleaning the house or doing grocery do not really increase your professional productivity but are nonetheless

important. You need food to eat and think clearly and if you will not do your grocery, you will keep ordering burgers and pizzas and as you know, junk food does not benefit your body or mind. Make sure you set a day of the week to attend to all the different tasks that do not directly relate to your goal but those you cannot completely ignore.

8. Go through your plan a few times and make any necessary changes as needed.

Go through this plan each night before going to bed and make any changes to it wherever you feel necessary. For instance, if something unexpected comes up and you need to meet a potential investor prior to dispatching a few orders as you had planned the next day, do the urgent task first. It is important to create a flexible plan and revisit it regularly so you can make necessary changes according to the need of the hour. This makes the plan more effective. With your plan ready, it is time to take some action. On the conclusion I have listed examples of useful productivity planners you can use in order to maximize the results.

The next section will focus on how to fight the urge to procrastinate so you can, like Nike, ***Just Do It!***

Procrastination is productivity's biggest enemy. It is what keeps you from living an impactful life or completing your work (and achieving your goals) as planned. To work on your plan of action, you MUST fight procrastination. If you fail to overcome procrastination, you will never achieve your goals as planned.

Here is how you can overcome the need to procrastinate and discipline yourself better.

.

Why You Procrastinate

"Mneh, I'll do it later." Procrastination has certain causes. If you find that cause and work to resolve it, you will no doubt beat procrastination. Here are some of the major reasons behind procrastination. Go through them a few times and then compare them with your situation to find out why you procrastinate

Now is not the Right Time to Do it: Most of us postpone tasks because we are always searching for the perfect time to do them. If you give the same reason each time you have something important to do, you need to understand that there is actually no perfect time to do something. Perfection is a myth and if you continue chasing it, you will never get anything done.

To get going, understand there is no perfect time or the perfect way to do something. Yes, there are times when 'you should strike the iron while it is hot' so you get best results and while there are effective ways to do different tasks, this should not keep you from taking action.

If you have a task to do, assess it and then figure out a suitable time to do it and then just do it. For instance, if you plan to exercise more to lose weight, figure out when you have some time to spare for this activity. If you are free in the evening, you could hit the gym at 5pm.

Too Difficult: Another major reason why we procrastinate is the challenging nature of a task. If a task seems too tough, you are likely to postpone it as much as possible. Instead of doing that, find out why a certain task appears difficult. Is it because you do not have the necessary skill to tackle it or is it because it is a huge task? If it is too big, chop it down into smaller steps as stated previously. If your reason for not working on a task is the lack of a skill, find out how you can develop that skill. For instance, if you need to create a beautiful cover for your book but do not have the necessary skills to do so, look for easy ways to do so online. When equipped with a skill that helps you do a task easily, you overcome the urge to defer that task to a later time.

I May Fail: Failure is a main reason why many of us put off our tasks. If you fear failing, you are likely not to want to do a certain task altogether. To overcome your fear of failure, understand that failure is just one side of the coin; success is the other.

To achieve success, you have to go through a few failures, which is perfectly fine. Failure is not here to weaken you; in fact, when well used, fear teaches you and grooms you for the impending success. Start seeing setbacks from this perspective and soon, you will feel more motivated to work on your tasks.

Too Boring: If a task seems too boring, you are likely to postpone it. If that is your reason for not doing certain activities, find interesting ways to do a task and peg interesting rewards to all the boring tasks. For instance, if you have to create a report, something you loath and consider boring, ask your best friend to keep you company, which will turn the task into an enjoyable experience. In addition, upon completing that task, you could reward yourself with a nice treat. Rewards increase your excitement about a task and thus make it easier for you to attend to it.

Find out why you procrastinate and then use the strategies given above to overcome the urge to procrastinate. When you feel ready to work, do the following to ensure you actually do your work and do not succumb to procrastination again.

Don't Overthink it

If you have a task to do, take 5 minutes to think of how to do it. If the task is too difficult, take a little more time but make sure you do not spend all your time thinking about it. When you overthink things, you suffer from analysis paralysis and fail to take any action. To keep yourself from falling into that trap, do not get into trivial details of how to do a task; just do it when you intend to work on it.

Try the 5-Minute Hack

This hack is an extremely effective way to overcome the urge to procrastinate and get stuff done fast. When you have a difficult task to complete but are not in the mood to do so, tell yourself "I will only do this task for 5 minutes." Since 5 minutes is not such a long time, you are likely to accept such a deal. When the 5 minutes are over, tell yourself, "let me do it for another 5 minutes." You will notice that in the first 2 5-minutes work intervals, you will feel motivated enough to keep going for more than 30 minutes to an hour. Continue working on the task and take a break once you have worked for 40 to 60 minutes. This hack tricks you into doing work and slowly increases your productivity.

Use the Pomodoro Technique

The Pomodoro technique is an effective time management strategy you can use to beat procrastination and increase your productivity. It is a tomato shaped time management tool based on a Pomodoro (Italian for tomato) shaped timer used by famous chef Francesco Cirillo.

Using this technique, you have to break a certain task into 3 or more parts of 30 to 35 minutes each. Next, work on one part and take a 5 to 10-minute break before moving on to the next installment. After doing the 4th part, you can take a longer break of 20~ minutes. This is especially important on tasks that require sitting, since you'll be able maintain better posture and therefore be more focused and vital. If you are working a lot sedentary, I'd personally suggest you start to research about posture in general. Anyway, back to topic. You must also review your work after each installment; this will help you, and then improve your performance. This technique breaks a big task into smaller chunks thus making it easier for you to attend to it and overcome your temptation to postpone it too.

Implement these strategies; if you do, you will find yourself doing your work instead of postponing it. To increase your motivation to keep doing your work as planned, always reward yourself after completing each task, boring or not.

Your next task is to increase your level of focus so you do things effectively and escalate your output.

Here's an image to demonstrate ideal environment for computer work. Remember to keep an eye on your posture, it's well researched that our bodies can't go longer than 50-60minutes of sitting in a naturally proper posture. Also, too long periods of sitting often tire you out both physically and mentally. This is obviously not what we want when trying to be as productive as possible.

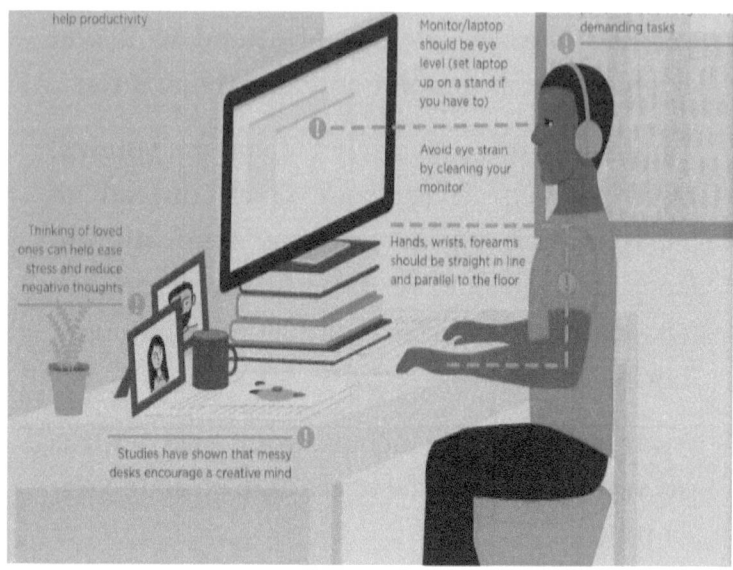

To ensure you stay on track and do your important tasks on time, you need to have killer focus. Increased focus ensures you keep increasing your productivity with each passing day and do not lose hope in difficult times. Here is how you can increase your level of focus.

Manage Distractions

It is difficult to stay focused when you are around distractions. If you have a mouth-watering pizza in front of you, you are likely to devour it instead of eating a bowl of salad. Similarly, if your friend pops in just as you are about to sit to work and asks you to accompany him/her for a movie, it is highly unlikely that you will say no to him/her.

Distractions weaken your focus and make it difficult for you to do the meaningful stuff. To experience increased focus, you absolutely must manage distractions.

To do that, create a list of all the different things, people, and activities that distract you from your work and lower your productivity. Next, write a few strategies you can use to combat each distraction effectively. If your friend has a bad habit of visiting you every day and sidetracking you from your work, you could tell him/her to stop visiting you during your work hours, you could stop taking his/her calls for a while, or you could go to your parent's house to focus on an important project. In a work situation, you can put a 'do not disturb' label outside your door, put on earphones even when you are not listening to anything etc. to discourage people from disturbing you. If you get distractions from internet usage e.g. you watch YouTube videos too much or spend too much time on various social networks, you can use tools like Leechblock or StayFocusd to limit your access to the sites that sidetrack you. These are just ideas; feel free to brainstorm what works best for you depending on your distraction.

Each time a certain distraction pops up, first remind yourself of what you should really be doing. Bring the bigger picture in your head and focus on it for a few moments. Think of why you have embarked on this journey in the first place and use those reasons to stimulate yourself to say no to your distractions even if it is yourself. Next, implement the strategies you chose earlier.

Make sure you say no to yourself each time you feel the urge to do something less meaningful. You could lure yourself into doing an important task by setting a reward you will enjoy only after completing the important task first.

Stop Multitasking

If you are in the habit of tackling more than one task at a time, this is why your focus is poor and productivity wanting. When you do more than one activity at a time, you keep your mind distracted. When your attention goes to one too many tasks simultaneously, you are less likely to do anything successfully. To become more focused and less distracted, stop multitasking.

Instead of doing several tasks at one time, focus on one task first. If you have to create a book cover, do it first, and after, review the

2,000 words you wrote today instead of moving back and forth between both tasks. To focus fully on one task, immerse yourself in it by focusing on every step. If you are creating a book cover, see how a color feels as you add it to the cover and how a certain image brings your cover to life. Take interest in every task and immerse yourself in it so you do it with complete attention.

Take Mini Breaks

It becomes difficult to focus when you work crazily for long hours without giving your mind and body any rest. When you work your mind and body, they get tired and when they get super-exhausted, you are less likely to focus on a task. To stay focused and energized, schedule mini breaks as you start a task. Take a small 5-minute break after working for every 30 to 40 minutes and take an hour or flexible break after you have done a few important tasks.

Do Something Fun

Make sure you do something fun and relaxing every day. Here's just some ideas:

Fun

- Exercise
- Eat out
- Meet people
- Travel
- Watch videos, movies, series
- Play games

Relaxing

- Meditate
- Laugh
- Look at the goals you have already achieved
- Cold or warm shower, sauna
- Stretching, Yoga
- Visualize the realized goals

- Whatever it is, remember it is important to leave little personal time as:

This gives you a break from the hectic work schedule and ensures you relax your mind before moving on to your difficult tasks. Fun activities increase your emotional well-being; when you feel happy and relaxed, you can work with increased energy and concentration.

Create a list of activities you enjoy doing and make you do at least one of them daily even if it is for just 15 minutes.

Work on these techniques and soon, you will find yourself working with increased focus. To make sure you fulfill your goals as planned, work on improving your level of self-discipline. The next section has great advice on how to do that.

Drink Coffee

Caffeine is the active ingredient in coffee that accounts for the mental boost. It achieves this by fitting into adenosine receptors, present throughout the body. Drinking a cup of coffee can temporarily boost your focus and energy levels. The key for using coffee to achieve long-term results however, is moderation.

A 2013 study on self-discipline conducted by Wilhelm Hoffman shows that those with high level of self-discipline are happier than those whose level of self-discipline is low because a high level of self-discipline gives you the ability to deal with goal conflicts effectively and do what is important.

To ensure you keep procrastination at bay and keep escalating your productivity, work on increasing your self-discipline. While all the strategies discussed previously certainly help you build and increase your discipline, here are a few more techniques you should use to skyrocket your level of discipline.

Become Process Oriented

You succumb to temptations and obstacles and give in to temptations because you focus on the end goal instead of the process that leads you to your goal. Being goal-oriented is great because it helps you focus better on the bigger picture. Being process-oriented is even better because it ensures that upon encountering obstacles, you do not give up or in. Instead, you acknowledge all your little accomplishments; this leaves you feeling proud and motivated to keep going.

To increase your level of discipline, become process-oriented. Get into the habit of, at the end of the day, reviewing your entire day's work and going through all your mistakes and any accomplishments. Appreciate yourself for what you did right and successfully, and find out how you can improve upon the things you failed at. Soon, you will find yourself becoming more involved in the process and doing meaningful tasks that move closer you closer to your ultimate goal.

Forgive Yourself

Ups and down are a part of the success process. If you want to be successful, you have to move forward even when after experiencing a setback. It is quite easy to slip into negative thinking and lose discipline when things fail to pan out as planned. To ensure that does not happen, forgive yourself each time you falter and encounter a setback and get back up. Look for any lessons you learned from the setback and tell yourself that you will improve the next time and will not keep wallowing. Also, say kind things to yourself such as "It is okay; it is not the end of the world," and "I am sure I'll do it better next time." Such thoughts rekindle your spirits to work on your goal.

Exercise

Exercise is most certainly a great way to improve your focus, increase your stamina, and make yourself feel happier and more excited about life in general and your goal in particular. It does so by increasing the production of mood improving hormones such as dopamine and serotonin that also increase your self-confidence. To stoke your confidence as well as stay on track to achieving your goals, you must exercise habitually.

You do not have to begin by hitting the gym for an hour every day. Just find any vigorous activity you enjoy doing and start doing it for

10 minutes every day. If you enjoy swimming, swim for 10 minutes daily. If you like dancing, engage in vigorous dancing for 10 minutes every day. Once you get into the habit of exercising for 10 minutes, increase the duration by 2 minutes every week until you can exercise for 60 minutes.

Surround Yourself with the Right People

It is easier to lose your determination to accomplish your goal when you are in an environment that supplies a steady stream of negativity. If your social circle is choke full of naysayers, no wonder you cannot manage your temptations. To stay disciplined and focused, surround yourself with positive people who inspire you, motivate you, and remind you of the importance of fulfilling your goals.

First, determine the naysayers in your company and then slowly distance yourself from them. As you do that, increase your interaction with the influential people and learn from their life experiences.

Leave Positive Notes Everywhere

Write down a few positive quotes and inspirational statements on a few post-its and pin them up at different places of your house and workplace. You could pin one on your bathroom mirror, another on your nightstand, one on your kitchen counter and so on. This way, you will surround yourself with positivity and every now and then, you will come across inspirational stuff that will remind you of your goal and will encourage you to keep fighting your temptations.

Sleep on Time

When your body is tired, it becomes difficult to think clearly and do what is right. If you find it tough to do what is important daily, analyze how much you sleep. If you sleep for less than 7 hours daily, this could be a major reason why you lack discipline. To feel active and focused, adults need an average of 7 to 9 hours of sleep every day. If you are sleeping for fewer hours, you need to do something to improve.

Set a sleep time and make sure you hit the bed at that exact same time daily. Secondly, create a soothing bedroom environment by making sure the room temperature is right, the bed is comfortable enough, and there are no noisy appliances in the room. Switch off your phone before you sleep so you do not stay glued to it. Also, ensure that your bedroom is dark, as this helps you get high quality sleep.

Make these strategies part of your life and sure enough, you will nurture the level of discipline you need to actualize all your goals.

"the expert in anything was once a beginner"

Conclusion, what's next?

We have come to the end of the book. Thank you for reading and congratulations! You made it here. This proves you're actually motivated enough to make it. Don't stop here. Continue and I'm certain you'll succeed in whatever you are after. Now take a short break if needed.

... are you back? Great, let's wrap this up. It's Christmas soon after all, yeah unless you're reading this on January, February... hmm.

Improve your focus and productivity, and you can achieve anything. This book has imparted upon you the knowledge you need to increase your focus and discipline. The onus is upon you now. Use this information to change your life and achieve all your goals. What's next you may ask?

Here are some tools to keep you going, just keep this in mind: don't get lost in all the available information. Your number one focus is always to take smart action. Reading books and studying basics is essential, but don't forget to take ACTION! Whatever you'll goals are you'll achieve them through action-based progress.

Talking of action, I've a small practical challenge to you. Take everything you learnt and apply it to your daily life for the next 30 days. Stick to it no matter what and see what happens!

Productivity planning

Clean & right size to carry with you if needed. There's plenty of these productivity planners online or in physical stores, don't use too much time for this. Alternatively, you can document similar planning on a google, word document or simply on paper / notebook. The main point here is that it is rather important to write down the goals you set for yourself

Remember tools like Leechblock and StayFocusd etc. if you are having trouble staying focused when working on your computer.

Simple description on what these apps do in a nutshell:

"Leech Block is a simple productivity tool: an extension for browsers designed to block those time-wasting sites that can suck the life out of your working day. All you need to do is specify which sites to block and when to block them.

You can specify up to six sets of sites to block, with different times and days for each set. You can block sites within fixed time periods (e.g., between 9am and 5pm), after a time limit (e.g., 10 minutes in every hour), or with a combination of time periods and time limit (e.g., 10 minutes in every hour between 9am and 5pm)." *One more bonus productivity hack: Consider listening to audiobooks or podcasts while walking, driving or doing basic house work.*

Finally. If, you found the book valuable, consider recommending it to others. One way to do that is to post a review. You can think of it as the first step on being productive. Just kidding, but whether it's to help me improve the book's content even further or just recommending it to others to benefit from, it's highly appreciated.

Thank you and best of luck! Stay productive and remember to enjoy life.

"We are what we repeatedly do. Excellence, then, is not an act, but a habit."   *- Aristotle 384 – 322 B.C*